GROW GIRL

This book is dedicated to my husband and children for all their support. To my parents whose love and protection helped me to accept the same from our Lord Jesus, and to my three sisters. Rosalind, Jessica, and Gloria who never let me give up!

TABLE OF CONTENTS

INTRODUCTION

As women, when it comes to our families we will do whatever it takes. When it comes to us there is always tomorrow. Why is it when the Lord is tugging at our hearts to pursue our dreams and visions we hesitate? Some of us come to a complete stop without realizing we could add so much more to our lives if in the morning we rose with the truth found in this statement made by the Apostle Paul, *"For I can do everything through Christ, who gives me strength."* Philippians 4:13. What does this mean? It means you can be a daughter, sister, aunt, wife, mother, grandmother and the woman God created you to be.

Although you may be accomplishing great things in one area of your life, you still may face feelings of being unfulfilled in life. *"So I came to hate life because everything done here under the sun is so troubling. Everything is meaningless-like chasing the wind."* Ecclesiastes 2:17. This comes as a direct result of not doing the things you were predestined, born to do. When you have been predestined by God "to do", goals and visions become a necessity not just a passing idea or thought. *"For God is working in you, giving you the desire and the power to do what pleases him,"* Philippians 2:13. If you are a woman whose identity has been built around what you do rather than who you are I encourage you to read on. Learn how you can join the many others who are now becoming the women God created and predestined them to be. As you read, read each chapter asking yourself these two questions:

- *Who does God say I am?*
- *What does God want to accomplish through my life?*

Your situation is not hopeless and the pain of your past is not fatal. All you need to do is believe God.

> *"Just then a woman who had suffered for twelve years with constant bleeding came up behind him. She touched the fringe of his robe, for she thought, "If I can just touch his robe, I will be healed." Jesus turned around, and when he saw her he said, "Daughter, be encouraged! Your faith has made you well." And the woman was healed at that moment.*
>
> *Matthew 9:20-22*

In this scripture it is the woman's belief that healed her. Perhaps you feel as if your case is hopeless or your dream is dead. Find hope in these words written in Matthew 9:18, 23-25.

> *"...My daughter has just died," he said, but you can bring her back to life again if you just come and lay your hand on her." "When Jesus arrived at the official's home, he saw the noisy crowd and heard the funeral music. Get out!" he told them. "The girl isn't dead; she's only asleep." But the crowd laughed at him. After the crowd was put outside,*

*however, Jesus went in and took the girl by
the hand, and she stood up!"*

Again, this father's belief, his faith is what allowed healing to
come. I am not asking you to ignore your past or your current
situation; instead I want you to face it by turning those
stumbling blocks into stepping stones.

In the first scripture the woman with the hemorrhage
had been sick a long time. She had used every resource
available to her. It was not until she got sick and tired of being
sick and tired that she went looking for the man she had heard
so much about. Many of you have heard about Jesus.
However, He is still just that to you, someone you have heard
about. In the second scripture (Matthew 9:18, 23-25) Jesus
spoke to the ruler and told him his daughter was not dead
only asleep. I want you to know the woman God created you
to be is not dead, she is only asleep. Some of your largest
issues are the result of surrounding yourself with and listening
to the wrong people. Take note in the second scripture, you
see the young maid was not awakened until Jesus cleared the
room. Sharing your dreams and visions with the wrong
people will cause you heartache. Possibly even cause your
dreams to die!

In Genesis read the story about Joseph and what
happened to him when he not only shared but trusted his
dream with his brothers. Joseph was betrayed and left to die.
Although Joseph was hurt and betrayed in his past, Joseph
spoke these words in reference to his future. "You intended
to harm me, but God intended it all for good. He brought me

to this position so I could save the lives of many people." Genesis 50:20. You see the things you experience in this life are not just about you. God doesn't just want to help you out, He wants to do great things in you so your life will impact lives around you.

As a young girl, I was molested twice by two total strangers who threatened to kill my family if I told. For years I kept these horrible ordeals to myself. I feared for the life of my loved ones, and I was ashamed. However, since letting go of my past and giving God my future I can say like Joseph, *"God intended it for my good."* Ephesians 3:20 reads *"Now all glory to God, who is able, through his mighty power at work within us, to accomplish infinitely more than we might ask or think."* Paul gave Glory to God in spite of his past and you can too, when you touch God with your pain and allow His power to work in and through you.

I know for many women *"trust"* is an issue. It seems every time you dare to trust someone it results in your being hurt. But as you read on I want to challenge you to do just that, *trust.* According to the Merriam Webster online dictionary, trust is to have *assured reliance on the character, ability, strength, or truth of someone or something.*

As you read on I will make many references to scripture because I believe we find our healing in the Word of God. Whoever you are, whatever you've done, wherever you have been, I want you to know you can start all over. This is not simply a process, but a lifestyle. This is something I have lived and continue to live each day. So sit back relax and *"Grow Girl."*

For I know the plans I have for you," says the Lord. "They are plans for good and not for disaster, to give you a future and a hope."

Jeremiah 29:11

Chapter One

Who Does God Say I Am?

"I knew you before I formed you in your mother's womb. Before you were born I set you apart and appointed you as my prophet to the nations." Jeremiah 1:5

It is safe to say before you or anything else can begin to grow, you must identify what it is and in this case who you are. Everything and everyone has a diet or process that must be followed in order to be what or whom they are to become. You do not nurture a foot in the same manner you nurture an arm. You do not feed an infant the same texture of food you feed a teenager. So before you can grow girl you must accept who you are and whose you are. The best way to determine who you are is to return to your Creator, God.

Depending on your convictions you might ask "how would God know who I am?" God had to remind Jeremiah who he was when He called him. He said He not only *knew* Jeremiah but He set him apart as His spokesman to the world. In John 1:48, Nathaniel asked *"How do you know about me?" Jesus replied, "I could see you under the fig tree before Philip found you."*

I believe the Lord has not taken time to create each of you just because He had nothing better to do. I am convinced everything and everyone is created with purpose. Even though you may not be able to see or comprehend what that purpose might be, it is still so! Ephesians 1:45 reads,

"Even before he made the world, God loved us and chose us in Christ to be holy and without fault in his eyes. God decided in advance to adopt us into his own family by bringing us to himself through Jesus Christ. This is what He wanted to do, and it gave him great pleasure."

So who are you? You are the woman God chose before He formed the world to be His spokesperson. You are the woman who despite some of the bad decisions and questionable choices, God chose. You are the woman that despite your past God has promised a future of greatness. Now you are probably asking the question, why me?

"The Lord did not set his heart on you and choose you because you were more numerous than other nations, for you were the smallest of all nations! Rather, It was simply that the Lord loves you, and he was keeping the oath he had sworn to your ancestors.

Deut. 7:7-8a

In other words He chose you for who He created you to be. So who are you? You are the woman God chose simply because He loves you. You have and will encounter many things in this life that will want to form you, however the Apostle Paul wrote, *"But you are not like that, for you are a chosen people..."* 1 Peter 2:9a. Because you have been chosen by God you no longer have to settle for just anything.

13

You do not have to give in to the pain of your past. You do not have to accept your past as part of your future. Why, because you have been created for *Greatness!*

So then what does it mean when you encounter hardship, hurt, and pain? What do you do after you have made wrong choices and bad decisions? Does it mean God does not love you? Does it mean you give up? Does it mean you should turn away from God? No. Regardless of your past and your response to God's love for you in your past, God has chosen you and He is allowing these things to shape you into a woman He can use. The Apostle Paul asked this question:

> *"Can anything ever separate us from Christ's love? Does it mean he no longer loves us if we have trouble or calamity, or are persecuted, or hungry, or destitute or in danger, or threatened with death? (As the Scriptures say, "For your sake we are killed every day; we are being slaughtered like sheep.") No, despite all these things, overwhelming victory is ours through Christ, who loved us. And I am convinced that nothing can ever separate us from God's love. Neither death nor life, neither angels nor demons, neither our fears for today nor our worries about tomorrow - not even the powers of hell can separate us from God's love. No power in the sky above or in the earth below - indeed, nothing in all creation*

will ever be able to separate us from the love
of God that is revealed in Christ Jesus our
Lord. "

Romans 8:35-39

Everything you encounter in this life has been allowed in order to stretch you and shape you into the woman God predestined you to be. Yes, you were predestined, your life is predestined and therefore it does not matter what you have done in the past. When you make a conscious decision to trust God then every plan He has for you is released to come to you. So, who are you? You are the woman who declares despite ALL you have gone through, ALL you are going through, and ALL you may go through, you will not let anything or anyone separate you from the God who loved you even before you loved Him.

Each time you read Jeremiah 1:5 know that the Lord is talking about you. Your life was predestined so that YOU would be a prophet — *an effective or leading spokesman!* You are here to make a difference. So when you are confronted by your past say to yourself *"You intended to harm me, but God intended it (every person who has hurt you, every bad decision) all for good..."* Genesis 50:20a. Just knowing the truth is not enough. You must recognize and accept God's truth regarding you. Isn't it amazing how we acknowledge others truth about us but find it difficult to accept God's truth, our Creators truth about our lives? Will you accept the truth that your loving Father, your Creator would never allow pain to come upon you except to use it as

He shapes you into the woman He predestined you to be? Knowing the truth will give you a sense of joy, peace and relief. It's like the little boy who sees his mama baking a cake; knowing she is baking a cake gives him an expectation of satisfaction. Eating the cake gives him the satisfaction. Knowing there is a God can provide you with a sense of healing, protection, forgiveness and hope. However, *knowing* God allows you to receive the healing, protection, forgiveness and hope that only He can give.

So look at your life and ask yourself, do I live a life that says I really know Him, or does my life say I know of Him? Does my life, my actions say I trust Him? In other words have you given God control of your life? Do you trust Him enough to believe that He has your best interests at heart even through the bad times? Do you trust Him enough to allow His plan for your life to become your plan for your life, even when those plans are scary, unpleasant, and unpopular? What is your real truth? Are you mad about something that happened in your past and now those unresolved feelings are pouring out all over your life? Do you see life through the lens of rejection, isolation, betrayal? What's really going on and what are you willing to do to change, to grow, to have joy and not just be happy? Happiness changes based on outward situations, but joy remains despite life's difficulties. So, what are you willing to do to be who God says you are? This is a familiar question yet it is both a simple and difficult question. Why? Because you can't make the changes necessary to grow all by yourself. If you're really going to grow and be your best self, you're going to have put on some things, and take off or remove some things. You're going to have to surround yourself with people who see in you and want the best for you as well as let go of those who do not. Yes, it's a simple yet difficult question. But if you want the best for your life then you're going to have to grow girl and you can't do that surrounded by and hanging onto negative thoughts and negative people. Let it go, and grow girl.

Pray with me:

> Jesus,
> I ask you to forgive me of my sins. Lord I need you to heal my hurts. Father, help me to live a life driven by my purpose, which is your plan for me. Help me to lay down everything and anyone that I am allowing to hold me back from being and doing what you created me to do. Show me my life's purpose and develop in me what it takes to fulfill my life's purpose. In Jesus' name I pray, AMEN.

WHO DOES GOD SAY I AM?

This chapter asks the question "Who Does God say I Am"? Take a moment to reflect on what you have read and then write a statement to dispel every lie the enemy has used to manipulate you, causing you not to embrace your value.

_____

_____

_____

_____

_____

_____

_____

_____

_____

_____

_____

_____

_____

_____

_____

_____

_____

_____

_____

_____

_____

_____

AFFIRMATIONS FOR MY LIFE

Now take a moment to search the scriptures and write affirmations declaring God's truth over your life.

_____

_____

_____

_____

_____

_____

_____

_____

_____

_____

_____

_____

_____

_____

_____

_____

_____

_____

_____

_____

_____

_____

_____

_____

_____

_____

_____

Chapter Two

What Does God Want To Accomplish Through Your Life?

For I know the plans I have for you," says the Lord. "They are plans for good and not for disaster, to give you a future and a hope."
Jeremiah 29:11

What does it mean when the God who created heaven and earth says He has a plan for your life but you are having difficulty just getting through each day? What does it mean when He says He has given you an expected end but you don't know if you will make it to tomorrow with all that is going on today? You see His thoughts are not the same as yours, and His way of doing things you can not comprehend. Isaiah 64: 8 reads "And yet, O LORD, you are our Father. We are the clay, and you are the potter. We all are formed by your hand."

What I remember about pottery class is each time a bubble or issue popped up the potter (me) beat the bubble out of the clay pushing it down to its original state of nothing and then beginning the process of shaping and molding again. Despite what was before me I knew in my heart it was a beautiful vase and once it was completed it would be a gift my mother would cherish always. Despite your past, even your present, you are going through the same process. You find yourself wanting to change, to grow, but somehow you keep finding yourself in a pit. In spite of the ferris wheel you seem to be on, you don't have to worry, don't be discouraged. Just as I knew what that lump of clay was going to become and was committed to seeing it take its shape and form, the Lord is doing the same. Even though you don't know who you are, God does and He is doing with you what I was doing with that clay. He is shaping and forming you into the person He predestined you to be. And yes, when it is all said and done you will find yourself living a victorious life for Him, and He too, just like my mom will be proud of the vessel you have become. Keep in mind He is the potter and you are the clay and He has a plan for your life.

More than likely you have heard and possibly even believed you can be anything or do anything you want if you just apply yourself. If this statement were only true... the truth is...if you were created to be a tree you will never be a rock. If you were created to be a doctor you will never be fulfilled as a nurse. Yes, there will be some good days when you think being a nurse is just fine. But there will be other days when the thought of being a nurse and not a doctor will become so overwhelming that you will want to just give up. You may look like a fish, act like a fish, even smell like a fish, but if you were created to be a dancer you are just that, a smelly dancer! Whatever or whomever you were created to be will come with a process. With this process will come pain, pressure and prosperity. So be comforted with these words *"Yet what we suffer now is nothing compared to the glory he will reveal to us later."* Romans 8:18. This is why despite your past, your challenges, bad decisions, the divorce, the abortion, the layoff, and the wayward children, God has a plan. However, the only way you will see God's plan for your life come to life is to endure the process. Yes, there will be times when you will have to take one for the team, team _____ (put your name here).

Be confident in knowing that God's plan for your life does not change based on your circumstances. God's love for you does not change just because you make a wrong turn on the road of life. Trust Him and make up your mind to grow girl. Really, what do you have to lose except for pain, pressure, guilt, and shame?

Take a look at the events in the life of Job. The Bible states Job was a perfect and upright man who loved God and hated evil. The Bible goes on to say Job was the richest man in his area. The scripture tells us the enemy believed the only reason Job trusted God was because of how rich he was. In other words satan did not believe Job served God for who He was. He believed Job only served God for what He had given him, family, a home, and riches. With God's permission, yes, His permission, the enemy was permitted to bring pain into Job's life. Why? Because the Lord knew Job and the plans He had for Job's life. He knew that placing Job on the potter's wheel would only cause Job to become Greater. So the scripture details that after his cattle, servants and children were killed Job trusted God, and because he did the Bible says *"...the Lord blessed Job in the second half of his life even more than in the beginning"* Job 42:12a. You see you can't go wrong when you make up your mind to serve God before, during, and after your struggles. Yes, life comes with ups and downs for everyone but when we choose to grow in the midst of our pain we become who we were created to be, and not what life's circumstances would dictate.

Have you ever taken inventory of your life and thought back on the ever popular question what do you want to be when you grow up? Only to find out you're all grown up and you are not who or what you wanted to be. You may be very successful in what you are doing, but at what cost? *"Hope deferred makes the heart sick, but a dream fulfilled is a tree of life."* Proverbs 13:12. Have you sold out your soul who you are in order to gain riches or love from someone who really isn't worthy of your love? Take a look inside and really ask yourself *what is my purpose? Who was I created to be? What was I created to do? What is my truth?* These questions are not meant to be deep, but to cause you to look past what you've always done towards what you ought to be doing. All too often we think it is our past, our circumstances, our spouse, our boss, our finances holding us back. Society wants you to believe that a father not being present 25 years ago, or perhaps a rape 10 years ago, even a spouse who walked out five years ago are the reasons you feel the way you do. Woman of God, it is not your past that dictates your future. It is your NOW! Paul says in Acts 20:24a, *"But my life is worth nothing to me unless I use it for finishing the work assigned me by the Lord Jesus..."* God created you on purpose, with purpose, for purpose.

As women we allow many things to shape who we are. There are four influences in particular that are given this privilege: our parents, our children, our spouses (significant other), and our careers. Society has programmed you to believe how well you do in these four areas will determine whether or not you are considered successful. Society says if you are a good child (obedient to your parents, teachers, etc.), if you do well in school (obtaining a degree), marry a good man, and land a good job (or own your own business) then you are successful. All of this is great unless you neglect the two essential components of success "Christ & Purpose." So then ask yourself "How do I become a woman God can use? How do I live the life God purposed for me so that I can not only do what God has purposed for me but I can have what God has purposed for me?

Pray with me:

> Jesus,
>
> I thank you for forgiving me of my sins and healing me of my hurts. Lord I want to be a woman you can use. I ask you now to take my past and my present and use it to mold me into that woman. The woman you had in mind when you created me. I surrender my past, present and future to you. In Jesus' name I pray, AMEN.

WHAT DOES GOD WANT TO ACCOMPLISH THROUGH YOUR LIFE?

This chapter asks the question "What Does God Want To Accomplish Through Your Life"? Take a moment to reflect on what you have read and then write a statement describing the gifts and talents you have been blessed with. The things that seem to come natural to you.

_____
_____
_____
_____
_____
_____
_____
_____
_____
_____
_____
_____
_____
_____
_____
_____
_____
_____
_____
_____
_____
_____
_____

AFFIRMATIONS FOR MY LIFE

Now take a moment to search the scriptures and write affirmations declaring God's truth over your life.

_____

_____

_____

_____

_____

_____

_____

_____

_____

_____

_____

_____

_____

_____

_____

_____

_____

_____

_____

_____

_____

_____

_____

_____

_____

Chapter Three

Becoming A Woman God Can Use

"For God knew his people in advance, and he chose them to become like his Son, so that his Son would be the firstborn among many brothers and sisters. And having chosen them, he called them to come to him. And having called them, he gave them right standing with himself. And having given them right standing, he gave them his glory." Romans 8:29-30

In becoming a woman God can use there is no need to be perfect. God can and will work through anyone. Despite the popular quote "you can't judge a book by its cover," we not only judge others from the outside we also judge ourselves from the outside. Rarely do you take the time to see yourself through the eyes of the Lord. In order to see yourself as God does, you must accept that He has a plan for your life and the life of those around you. You must accept yourself and others for who He created each to be. When the scripture declares you are "wonderfully complex" in Psalm 139:14, He was not speaking only to you, He was speaking to all who would listen. The sooner you recognize and accept the Lord knows you, He knows where you have been, where you are, and most importantly where you are going, it will become easier to accept yourself and others without judgment. In Exodus 3:11 Moses pondered many of the questions you find yourself asking God today. "Who am I?" Experiences in life will cause many to ask this question. Remember what the Lord wants to accomplish through you is not about you. It is about others coming to know Him through you.

In becoming a woman God can use you must remind yourself that your life is about living for God and not yourself. As women, the fact we are gifted in so many areas tends to be one of our major downfalls. In being so gifted we sometimes neglect to consult the Lord before acting. In the familiar poem entitled *"A Letter From God,"* the writer puts into words God's love and yearning to be in a relationship with His creation...you. The writer notes while the Lord is waiting for His creation to acknowledge Him, He chooses to bless him. In Revelation Jesus spoke these words *"Look! I stand at the door and knock. If you hear my voice and open the door, I will come in..."* Revelation 3:20a. You see, the Lord desires to be a part of your life. The question is will you find the time in your busy schedule to let Him in?

Do you find yourself doing everything you feel you are expected to do and nothing God has purposed you to do? When was the last time you spent private time with the Lord? Time you set aside the needs of others and sought Him for you and you alone. He wants to use your human means and your natural abilities, your brokenness and your pain to accomplish great and mighty acts. The unspoken needs, desires, dreams, and visions of your heart are not just decisions you made each time someone asked you "what do you want to be when you grow up?" These desires were placed in you while you were in your mother's womb. God says *"It is the same with my word. I send it out, and it always produces fruit. It will accomplish all I want it to, and it will prosper everywhere I send it"* Isaiah 55:11. He wants to use you. He does not want you to depend upon your own strengths and ability. He does not want you to allow the pain of your past to dictate your future.

If somehow you can believe God created you with purpose and He indeed has a plan for your life, your next question will probably sound something like "what do I have to offer?" My finances are a wreck, my children are out of control, and all these things are weighing heavily on my marriage, my life. It is amazing how much you miss when you look at yourself through your own eyes. *"...No eye has seen, no ear has heard, and no mind has imagined what God has prepared for those who love him"* 1 Corinthians 2:9. When you look at your life's circumstances with your natural eye you see your past, and definitely your failures. When you look at your life's circumstances through the eyes of Christ, what you see will be extraordinary! You will see a mighty woman of God who He describes in the scriptures as being fearfully and wonderfully made. The next time you begin to ask the questions "who am I, what do I have to offer?" you can look at David.

When you read the scriptures you will see King David did not always act like a King. David was not acting like a king when he was chosen to be king. If David with all his struggles could be called a man after God's own heart, then surely there is room at the cross for you and me. When you see yourself through the eyes of the Lord you will then embrace the woman God says you are. A woman, who has the faith to move mountains. The woman who according to John 15:7, knows if she lives in Christ and His word lives in her she can ask whatever she will and it *shall* be done.

One song writer penned the lyrics, "I am happy just to know that I am His child." When you come to know Jesus, His awesomeness begins to change you into a woman He can use. Knowing Him as Jehovah-Jireh your provider, will help you to believe no matter what you may have need of in this life He will provide. Knowing Him as Emmanuel will strengthen your belief to know no matter what you may be going through or what you may encounter, He is with you. Jehovah-Shalom will keep you in perfect peace when everything around you seems to be in chaos, and El Shaddai, The God who is sufficient for the needs of His people is more than enough no matter what life brings you. The woman God uses knows by whatever means she comes through it is not about her, God is just shaping the woman He says she is. So when the enemy comes against you, stand on the Word of God which declares *"This means that anyone who belongs to Christ has become a new person. The old life is gone; a new life has begun!"* 2 Corinthians 5:17.

There will be times when what God has predestined for you may seem impossible because of your past. Still when you accept God has a plan for your life you will know what you have done in the past is just that, the past. When you allow God to step in there is a change and that change allows you to become a woman He can use. What you once attempted to accomplish through intellect and failed, will now be accomplished through trusting God, relying only on His ability, His character, His strength, and His unfailing love for you.

Paul didn't always present himself as a servant of God. As a man defined and shaped by his society Paul, then called Saul was against and even killed those who confessed a love and belief in God the Father, and Jesus His Son. However God had a plan, and once again what the devil meant for bad, God used for His good. The story of Paul's experience on the road to Damascus (Acts 22) continues to impact lives today. Paul recognized after coming to know Jesus what he was going through was not about him but about God and what He wanted to do with Paul's life. So instead of looking at your circumstances as stumbling blocks see them as stepping stones towards where God is taking you. You may not understand the why but if you will trust Him with the why, the promise found in Isaiah 43:1-4 belongs to you.

"But now, O Jacob, listen to the Lord who created you. O Israel, the one who formed you says, "Do not be afraid, for I have ransomed you. I have called you by name; you are mine. When you go through deep waters I will be with you. When you go through rivers of difficulty, you will not drown. When you walk through the fire of oppression, you will not be burned up; the flames will not consume you. For I am the Lord, your God, the Holy One of Israel, your Savior. I gave Egypt as a ransom for your freedom; I gave Ethiopia and Seba in your place. Others were given in exchange for you.

I traded their lives for yours because you are precious to me. You are honored, and I love you."

Pray with me:

Jesus,

I thank You for forgiving me. Father, help me to see myself and others as you do. As I go through the process of becoming a woman you can use help me to trust you and turn total control of my life over to You. In Jesus' name I pray, AMEN.

BECOMING A WOMAN GOD CAN USE?

"Becoming A Woman God Can Use" begins with owning your truth. Take a moment to reflect on what you have read. What characteristics have you taken on in response to your circumstances in life? What do you need to do to become a woman God can use?

_____

_____

_____

_____

_____

_____

_____

_____

_____

_____

_____

_____

_____

_____

_____

_____

_____

_____

_____

_____

_____

_____

_____

_____

AFFIRMATIONS FOR MY LIFE

Now take a moment to search the scriptures and write affirmations declaring God's truth over your life.

_____

_____

_____

_____

_____

_____

_____

_____

_____

_____

_____

_____

_____

_____

_____

_____

_____

_____

_____

_____

_____

_____

_____

_____

_____

_____

_____

_____

QUESTIONS

You may not be able to answer all of the following questions at this moment, but as you "GROW GIRL" you will...

1. Who does God say I am?

2. What does God want to accomplish through my life?

3. How would God know who I am?

4. What do you do when you encounter hardship, hurt and pain?

5. What does it mean to trust God?

6. What does it mean to obey God?

7. What is my purpose?

8. Who was I created to be?

9. What was I created to do?

10. How do I become a woman God can use?

NOTES

Chapter Four

Growing With Jesus

"Yes, I am the vine; you are the branches. Those who remain in me, and I in them, will produce much fruit. For apart from me you can do nothing." John 15:5

No matter how you look at it, whatever you experience in this life it is not about you. It is about what God wants to do in you, for you, and through you. The scripture declares in Acts 17:28a, *"For in him we live and move and exist…"* Your existence is because of Him, through Him, and for Him. As you begin to know Him better and grow in Him, you will understand He alone is the source of everything that is vital in your life. Your very heartbeat is dependent upon His breathing the breath of life into you each moment. As you seek God for the answers to your circumstances, your situations, and yes, your existence, you should listen with your heart and not your past or your pain. When you open yourself up to Him He will speak to you through His Word, through men and women of the gospel, and even through those circumstances that seem to overwhelm you right now. He will speak through the wind and the rain, your joy and *yes*, your pain. God is always speaking. Are you listening? You must release your control and your expectations to make room for His. Many times disappointment comes when you seek the Lord for answers because you already have your own expectations of what the answer should be. As you grow in God you must seek for His will and not your own. The only way to be the woman God has predestined you to be is to allow His will to become your will. "My thoughts are nothing like your thoughts," says the Lord, and my ways are far beyond anything you could imagine" Isaiah 55:8. Proverbs 16:25 says, *"There is a path before each person that seems right, but it ends in death."* Again, if you allow your past and how you feel to dictate your actions your dreams and visions will die.

As the woman God has chosen you must take responsibility for your actions as you seek and act upon God's plan for your life. In order to do this you must grow with Jesus. You must submit to a life of prayer, be committed to His will, and trust in the way He desires to accomplish His will in your life and the lives of those around you. In doing this it will become necessary to set boundaries for your life, otherwise it will not matter how good the attempt, you will fail. You have to know who is in control. You have to have a clear picture of who you are and whose you are. Your heart has to be receptive to what the will of the Lord is for your life. Psalm 119:9 reads *"How can a young person stay pure? By obeying your word."* It is the lie of society that will cause you to believe you can change yourself and even others around you. Your fight is not against flesh and blood. Although the enemy will use people to distract you; even harm you, defeating the person will never give you the satisfaction or growth you are looking for.

So how do you grow with Jesus? You grow with Him through prayer. *Talk to God...*He wants to know how much you love Him, how you are feeling, and what you need. Yes,

He is all knowing, but when you come to Him it is a reminder that you are totally reliant upon Him. *Read and obey His word.* In His word God reveals His thoughts and His character to you. He reveals to you the plan He has for you, and most importantly how you can accomplish the plan. *Fellowship (church).* You can grow by joining a support network of brothers and sisters. In praying and learning of God with those who have gone through, those who are going through, and those who believe God with you. *Through worship.* When you worship God you express His worth to you. Praise Him not only for what He has done, but praise Him for who He is. Humble yourself before Him and acknowledge that you can do nothing without Him. When you worship, your desire to submit to His will through obedience is made known.

Pray with me:

Jesus,

I thank You for for loving me.   Father, I thank you for never giving up on me, even when I wanted to give up on myself. Despite what I have gone through in this life I now have a desire to grow and to become the woman you predestined me to be. Help me as I crucify my flesh and allow your will to become my will.

In Jesus' name I pray,
AMEN.

GROWING WITH JESUS

"Growing With Jesus" is a matter of choice. Take a moment to reflect on what you have read and then write a statement to share what you are willing to do and Grow Girl!

_____

_____

_____

_____

_____

_____

_____

_____

_____

_____

_____

_____

_____

_____

_____

_____

_____

_____

_____

_____

_____

_____

_____

_____

AFFIRMATIONS FOR MY LIFE

Now take a moment to search the scriptures and write affirmations declaring God's truth over your life.

_____

_____

_____

_____

_____

_____

_____

_____

_____

_____

_____

_____

_____

_____

_____

_____

_____

_____

_____

_____

_____

_____

_____

_____

_____

_____

_____

_____

Chapter Five

Prayer: A Believer's Privilege

"The one thing I ask of the Lord- the thing I seek most- is to live in
the house of the Lord all the days of my life, delighting in the Lord's
perfections and meditating in his Temple." Psalm 27:4

As you grow with God you will come to appreciate prayer as a believer's privilege. It is a time of communicating with God and enjoying His presence. Prayer is a necessary nutrient in the life of the woman God uses. As you explore the scriptures you will find that Jesus considered time alone with His Father to be very important. There are numerous times recorded in the scriptures of how Jesus took time away from all He was doing to spend quality time in prayer. "Before daybreak the next morning, Jesus got up and went out to an isolated place to pray." Mark 1:35. Jesus knew the power He possessed was not a result of His own strength, but the result of being in right relationship with His Father. *"And a voice from heaven said, "You are my dearly loved Son, and you bring me great joy."* Mark 1:11

After being tempted Jesus went on to do great things in casting out demons and healing the sick. Jesus took no time to boast, He rose up early the next morning to pray. It does not matter what your agenda is for the day you should always take time to pray. When you spend time with the Lord in prayer you grow closer to Him and more like Him. You may encounter wilderness experiences, but when you rely on the strength of God you can accomplish much.

"But despite Jesus' instructions, the report of his power spread even faster, and vast crowds came to hear him preach and to be healed of their diseases. But Jesus often withdrew to the wilderness for prayer."

Luke 5:15, 16

When you really begin to understand the effort it takes to pray and the results obtained through prayer, you will begin to recognize prayer as a believer's privilege. In a time when most would be capitalizing on their fame, Jesus prayed. Jesus knew the importance of prayer. Jesus knew without a doubt prayer changes things. He knew the best way to remain in right relationship with His Father was the same as any other relationship, it is with communication, and in the case of our Heavenly Father, PRAYER. So whether things are going good, or the challenges of life are getting you down, prayer is the key.

It does not matter what you are facing. Jesus set the example when He demonstrated the power of prayer in the Garden of Gethsemane. Jesus knew His purpose. So instead of wasting time murmuring and complaining, He stopped to pray the will of the Father. Yes He made His request known, and He trusted His Father to know what was best for Him even in His last hours. Likewise you must recognize the privilege of prayer and pray. For if there is to be any change it will come as a result of prayer, communicating with the Father regarding His will for your life. Mary the mother of Jesus knew full well the ridicule she would face as the result of being the woman God had chosen yet she responded *"... I am the Lord's servant. May everything you have said about me come true."* Luke 1:38. Whatever you are going through, and whatever needs you may have Matthew 6:33 encourages you to *"Seek the kingdom of God above all else, and live righteously, and he will give you everything you need."* Whatever Jesus needed He went to His Father and His Father answered Him in prayer! Through prayer and the reading of God's word, God's will and His actions are revealed to you.

When you release yourself to God He is free to perform His will in your life. There can be many temporary solutions to the needs in your life but the blessings of God through prayer are eternal. Do not be fooled, as it is with most things we desire, prayer requires effort. Along with your spiritual desire to do right, there is the natural desire to do otherwise.

In prayer one of the most common answers is change and change is something the natural man does not enjoy. The challenge comes when trying to figure out what to pray.

> *"And the Holy Spirit helps us in our weakness. For example, we don't know what God wants us to pray for. But the Holy*
>
> *Spirit prays for us with groanings that cannot be expressed in words. And the Father who knows all hearts knows what the Spirit is saying, for the Spirit pleads for us believers in harmony with God's own will."*
>
> *Romans 8:26, 27*

What a mighty God! *First*, you benefit from prayer in that your praying brings you closer to the Father. *Next*, He answers your prayers and tells you to feel free to ask for whatever you want and it will come. *Last*, but definitely not least, even when you don't know what to pray for, all you need to do is make the effort and the words will come! So what are you waiting for? Prayer is a believer's privilege, why not use it! The fact you don't use this privilege reminds me of a poem written by an Unknown Author. The author details in simplicity the need to put forth effort if you want results. Unless you take time to pray, time to communicate with your Father, you will never discover the riches He has in store for you. You may never discover the truth of God's Word. The truth that says in spite of what is going on around you, you can depend on Jesus! When you pray you are relying on God's power to transform you. The very premise of prayer says that you can't handle the situation on your own, you need Jesus! In a song made popular by David Robertson the writer asks the Lord to hold him close as he says goodbye to living his life somewhere in between his love for himself and his love for God. Doesn't this sound like so many of us? We want to do the right thing, but it is so hard to say goodbye to me. Paul says it In Romans like this…

> *"And I know that nothing good lives in me,*
> *that is, in my sinful nature. "I want to do what*
> *is right, but I can't. I want to do what is good,*
> *but I don't. I don't want to do what is wrong,*
> *but I do it anyway."*
>
> *Romans 7:18, 19*

So you see God knows you are unable to change and sustain the change by yourself. The Lord knew change would not be easy and so He sent His Son and His Son gave His life just for you.

As a woman God can use you must give up having to have things your way and accept the challenge of building a closer relationship with Christ through prayer. Jesus demonstrated this in the midst of all He was doing by taking the time to pray. You must lay aside the dishes, the laundry, the children, the job, and the television to pray. Ask yourself, have I said goodbye to me? Relinquish your control and trust the only effort required on your part as you encounter conflict and choices is to surrender to God— for Prayer Is A Believer's Privilege.

Pray with me:

> Jesus,
> I thank You for the privilege of prayer. Father help me to trust you with all and for all. I want to be the woman you predestined me to be so help me to accept Your will as my will. In Jesus' name. I pray, AMEN.

PRAYER A BELIEVERS PRIVILEGE

"Prayer A Believers Privilege" – Prayer proves to be a benefit only if we use it. So many times the solution is right at our fingertips but we miss it. Take a moment to reflect on what you have read. How often have you faced the issues of life and failed to take them to God in prayer. This is your opportunity!

Father,_____

_____

_____

_____

_____

_____

_____

_____

_____

_____

_____

_____

_____

_____

_____

_____

_____

_____

_____

_____

_____

_____

_____

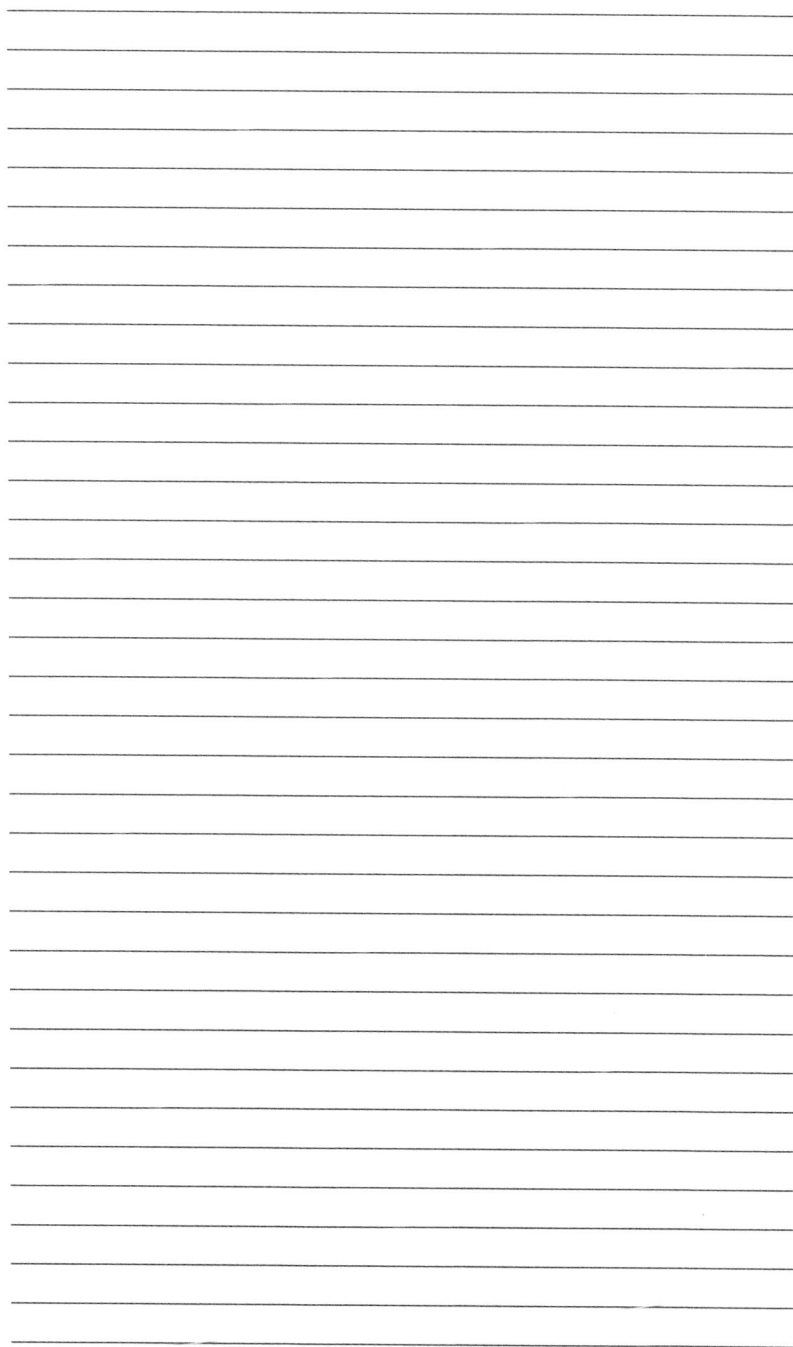

AFFIRMATIONS FOR MY LIFE

Now take a moment to search the scriptures and write affirmations declaring God's truth over your life.

_____

_____

_____

_____

_____

_____

_____

_____

_____

_____

_____

_____

_____

_____

_____

_____

_____

_____

_____

_____

_____

_____

_____

_____

_____

_____

_____

_____

_____

Chapter Six

Conflict and Choices

"I love God's law with all my heart. But there is another power within me that is at war with my mind. This power makes me a slave to the sin that is still within me." Romans 7:22-23

Conflict is one word we all would like to look past when discussing our lives. However, once you have made a choice to live for the Lord you are guaranteed to encounter conflict. As you read the beatitudes in Matthew 5, you are reminded of the blessings received as a direct result of the choices you make during conflict.

> *"God blesses those who realize they are poor and realize their need for Him, for the Kingdom of Heaven is theirs. God blesses those who mourn, for they will be comforted. God blesses those who are humble, for they will inherit the whole earth. God blesses those who hunger and thirst for justice, for they will be satisfied. God blesses those who are merciful, for they will be shown mercy. God blesses those whose hearts are pure, for they will see God. God blesses those who work for peace, for they will be called the children of God. God blesses those who are persecuted for doing right, for the Kingdom of Heaven is theirs. God blesses you when people mock you and persecute you and lie about you and*

say all sorts of evil things against you
because you are my followers. Be happy
about it! Be very glad! For a great reward
awaits you in heaven. And remember, the
ancient prophets were persecuted in the same
way."

Matthew 5:3-12

The Word of God assures you that in the midst of your conflict you are blessed. When your conflict, circumstances, and challenges are a direct result of your relationship with the Lord you can expect His reward. When conflict arises and there is a choice to be made, Jesus tells you to rejoice in these things. You have to stop trying to figure life out on your own, and let God be God!

When you are faced with conflict the first decision or choice you should make is to relinquish your will to God. When there is a choice to be made you must choose to be who God has created and predestined you to be. Who you are should not change from conflict to conflict. According to 1 John 4:4, whose you are will change the situation, *"But you belong to God, my dear children. You have already won a victory over those people, because the Spirit who lives in you is greater than the spirit who lives in the world."* When you face adversity or conflict you should be who God made you to be and not become the person the situation would like to change you into. As a woman, be the woman whose choices honor the Lord. No, at times it will not be easy, but it will be worth it, as you see the mighty woman of God coming forth, and the influence you have had on the lives around you.

It has been said over the years that the woman sets the tone for the home. Should this be true when a woman of God wants peace in her home she should demonstrate peace in the midst of the storm. She should project victory even when defeat is knocking at the door. The fact that you are in the storm does not say what manner of woman you are, it is how you go through and come out of the storm. In conflict will you choose the characteristics of the Proverbs 31 woman?

1 Peter 2:19-21 infers God is pleased with you when you patiently endure unfair treatment. This suffering is all part of what God has called you to and He is your example. In all that He suffered He never sinned or complained. Whenever conflict arose Jesus left His case in the hands of His Father who always judges fairly. In other words, He let God be God! The Lord is pleased when you are in right relationship with Him for it releases Him, no it moves Him to act on your behalf just as He demonstrated on the cross by forgiving the dying thief. In spite of what He Himself was facing this mans change of heart moved Jesus to act on his behalf. When you are faced with conflict all you need to do is pray and allow your need for Jesus to move Him to your rescue. It does not matter what choices you may have made in the past according to the Psalmist-

> *"He does not punish us for all our sins; he does not deal harshly with us as we deserve. For his unfailing love toward those who fear him is as great as the height of the heavens above the earth." Psalm 103:10, 11*

Once you return or come to God it is as if you had never sinned, been separated or left and He has a reward for you. So stop looking at your life through your past and stop attacking your circumstances with your own strength. Take a good look at Jesus and place your life in His hands. From conception to death, Jesus faced conflict and had to make choices. Likewise you can be sure that you will be challenged through conflict to make choices. However, if you meditate on the words found in Isaiah 43:18, 19 you will find comfort.

> *"But forget all that-it is nothing compared to what I am going to do. For I am about to do something new. See, I have already begun! Do you not see it? I will make a pathway through the wilderness. I will create rivers in the dry wasteland."*

The Lord, your Heavenly Father wants to do a new thing in your life so stand up and declare. *"For I can do everything through Christ, who gives me the strength"* Philippians 4:13.

Pray with me:

Jesus,

I know as I make this commitment to follow You and live a life dedicated to serving You I will be faced with conflict and choices. Help me to make decisions and choices that are in line with Your word and Your purpose for my life. Help me to let go of having things my way and trust You to know what is best for me. In Jesus' name. I pray, AMEN.

CONFLICT AND CHOICES

"Conflict and Choices" – We all have them. The issue isn't that we have them, it's what we do when we have them that determine our outcome. Take a moment to reflect on what you have read. How will you respond to conflict and choices as you grow girl?

_____

_____

_____

_____

_____

_____

_____

_____

_____

_____

_____

_____

_____

_____

_____

_____

_____

_____

_____

_____

_____

_____

_____

AFFIRMATIONS FOR MY LIFE

Now take a moment to search the scriptures and write affirmations declaring God's truth over your life.

_____

_____

_____

_____

_____

_____

_____

_____

_____

_____

_____

_____

_____

_____

_____

_____

_____

_____

_____

_____

_____

_____

_____

_____

_____

_____

_____

_____

_____

Chapter Seven

The Weight

"Therefore, since we are surrounded by such a huge crowd of witnesses to the life of faith, let us strip off every weight that slows us down, especially the sin that so easily trips us up. And let us run with endurance the race God has set before us."
Hebrews 12:1

There will be times in your walk with God when you will feel as if you are the only one experiencing life's challenges. There will also be times when you look around and think the whole world is falling apart. Everywhere you look it seems as if people are suffering, marriages are failing, finances are scarce, and health issues are off the charts. The attack of the enemy has come so strong many have become distracted from fulfilling their purpose. Even Christians have become so distracted by their circumstances they seem to have forgotten God has a plan, a plan that is revealed through those very circumstances. Remember it is during your walk through challenges your purpose is discovered and fulfilled.

Over the years many of us have read, recited, spoken on, and referred to Hebrews 12:1 with the focus being the sin. However, this passage also encourages you to strip off every thing that slows you down and hinders your progress. If you want to live a life of faith and fulfill your purpose you must not only forsake sin, you must take off every thing that hinders you. Your growth will not come just as a result of knowing God's word and His purpose for your life. You must take action. Obey His word. Otherwise, you are only fooling yourselves. If you listen to the word and don't obey, it is like glancing at yourself in a mirror. You see your hair is a mess. If you walk away without taking action your hair will remain a mess. James 1:22, 25 reads,

> *"But don't just listen to God's word. You must do what it says. Otherwise, you are only fooling yourselves." But if you keep looking carefully into the perfect law that sets you free, and if you do what it says and don't forget what you heard, then God will bless you for doing it."*

You see weights are easy to pick up during our lives and tough to let go, but it must be done. You must accept God's presence and His desire to be a vital part of your life so you can see Him for who He is and what He wants you to be. Understand He is a gentleman. If you do not make room or time for Him He will not force His way in. So you must ask yourself "am I doing the things God purposed me to do? Or am I doing the things He allows me to do?" Keeping in mind you were created with purpose, are the things that occupy your time and talents keeping you from fulfilling your purpose or are they helping you to fulfill your purpose? Will your daily routine and activities somehow help you reach your purpose? Let us look at the parable of the servants who were given talents (Matthew 25). If you recall for a time they were each allowed to do whatever they wanted with the talent(s) they were given. In the end the one who had received the one talent had his talent taken away because He did not make good use of what God had given him. So as you walk toward your purpose you can not allow weights, people or circumstances to cause you to take the easy road. The road that says it will never get any better than this, and I will never be more than I am right now.

Holding on to weights might allow you the opportunity to utilize your gifts occasionally, but they will never allow you to launch into the deep. What are the weights in your life? *Children?* Are you still doing the things for your young adult that you did for him as a young child? *Weight.* How about your home? Is your story like mine? I was always going to read my Word and pray *after* I folded the clothes, cleaned the kitchen, etc. *Weight.* How about the job? Have you decided to obtain worldly treasure and disregard eternal pleasure? Does it seem there is always a need to work late on Bible Study night? Does the company social always seem to be scheduled on a day that has been set aside to fellowship with God? *Weight.* Even Ministry. Are you so busy in ministry that you don't take time for personal ministry. So busy ensuring everyone else is receiving what it is they need from God that you don't make time for yourself to receive from Him. *Weight.* After carrying this weight for many years it finally dawned on me, there are only 24 hours in each day and if you give eight (8) of them to resting, eight (8) of them to working, depending on where you live a minimum of two (2) hours for transportation, four (4) to family time/extracurricular activities that means you have two (2) hours remaining to put towards God's purpose for your life. Two hours out of 24 available *for God if nothing else comes up*! I'm not saying these things are not important, but I am saying that with all you can be involved in you must make the time you have for God count. You must do the things that will push you towards fulfilling your purpose in God. These things will give you fulfillment in this life and an eternal reward in the life to come. Finding and giving time to the things of God will enhance your life. Spending time each day with God will give you the strength, courage, and peace needed to fulfill all the other things life will bring. Trust me if you desire to be a better woman, daughter, sister, aunt, mother, grandmother and wife, give God His time and watch Him transform your life and your outlook on life.

Take just a moment to throw out the trash (weight)

- I feel guilty of_____.
- I feel shame about_____.
- I am fearful of_____.
- I blame_____.

Pray with me:

> Lord,
>
> there are so many things I desire to do in my life, however the things I am already doing seem to weigh me down. Help me to lay aside all the things that I am doing that keep me from being the woman you created me to be. Help me to trust that if I give time to You and Your will for my life You will work all these other things out. In Jesus' name. I pray, AMEN.

THE WEIGHT

"The Weight" – Now it is time to identify those things that have kept you from becoming who you are predestined to be. Take a moment to reflect on what you have read. Make a list of the things you believe have weighted you down keeping you from growing into who God says you are.

_____
_____
_____
_____
_____
_____
_____
_____
_____
_____
_____
_____
_____
_____
_____
_____
_____
_____
_____
_____
_____
_____

AFFIRMATIONS FOR MY LIFE

Now take a moment to search the scriptures and write affirmations declaring God's truth over your life.

_____
_____
_____
_____
_____
_____
_____
_____
_____
_____
_____
_____
_____
_____
_____
_____
_____
_____
_____
_____
_____
_____
_____
_____
_____
_____

Chapter Eight

Launch Into The Deep

"Then I heard the Lord asking, "Whom should I send as a messenger to this people? Who will go for us?" Isaiah 6:8a

So what does it all mean? What happens after you recognize who God says you are? What happens after you realize *what God wants to accomplish through your life? What happens after you accept the challenge in becoming a woman God can use, you begin growing with Jesus, you utilize prayer as a believer's privilege, you embrace conflict and choices, and lay aside the weight?* It is time to launch into the deep!

What does it mean to launch into the deep? Let's begin by looking at the definition of the words launch and deep from the Merriam Webster Online Dictionary.

- Launch - to put into operation or set in motion, to spring forward
- Deep - extending well inward from an outer surface

So when I say launch into the deep, I am asking you to look deep inside yourself into your past and confront every pain, every bad decision, every wrong you have encountered in order to see the purpose for which God allowed these thing to happen.

In order to launch into the deep you must be brave enough to remember the last time you felt fulfilled, happy, complete. If you are familiar with a track runner, before the race begins the sprinter backs into the blocks in order to get in proper position to start the race. In like fashion you will need to first step back to be in proper position to move forward. To move toward the place you were predestined before you allowed the hurt of your past, the shaping of society, and the hopelessness that became your constant companion to set in. Reading this book is not coincidental just as your past was not coincidental. Everything that you and I have encountered was for a reason. No, I do not understand why I had to be molested, I do not know why my biological father walked away and never returned, I do not know why I had to suffer 3rd degree burns over my body, I do not know why the privilege of having my mother was taken away so early in my life, but what I do know is that everything I have gone through was designed for me to be the woman I am becoming. With every incident of your past you are given a choice. Read the scriptures found in Deuteronomy 30:15, 19.

> *"Now listen! Today I am giving you a choice between life and death, between prosperity and disaster. Today I have given you the choice between life and death, between blessings and curses. Now I call on heaven and earth to witness the choice you make. Oh, that you would choose life, that you and your descendants might live!"*

Whatever your decision may have been in the past; today as you complete this book you are being given another chance to make a different choice. So what will your choice be? Will you accept the pain of your past as a stepping stone and embrace the love Jesus has for you, knowing that all you have had to endure and all you will encounter is a direct result of His love for you. Remember these scriptures found in Joshua and Ephesians.

Study this Book of Instruction continually. Meditate on it day and night so you will be sure to obey everything written in it. Only then will you prosper and succeed in all you do. This is my command-be strong and courageous! Do not be afraid or discouraged. For the Lord your God is with you wherever you go.

Joshua 1:8, 9

Get rid of all bitterness, rage, anger, harsh words, and slander, as well as all types of evil behavior. Instead, be kind to each other, tenderhearted forgiving one another, just as God through Christ has forgiven you.

Ephesians 4:31, 32

Woman it is not about you! It was, has been and will always be about what God wants to do in you, for you and through you, so launch into the deep. Allow your pain and your past to provoke you to do something more with your future.

Launch into the deep and allow the favor of God to take you to places that can not be measured. A place even when things are not going well your joy and peace is not disturbed but your faith is increased.

Pray with me:

Jesus,

Lord to this point it has been fairly easy to trust and do but today as I confront my past and my pain I need You to help me. I need You Lord to go with me into the darkness so I may see the light of Your love. I give my past and everything that has come to blind me from the reason You created me to you. Help me Lord to put the past behind me and move forward to accomplish all the things You created me to do and to be the WOMAN You created me to be. In Jesus' name. I pray, AMEN.

LAUNCH INTO THE DEEP!

"Launch Into the Deep" is a command. If you have done the work it is time to launch! You may not have noticed, but you have Grown Girl! You are not the same woman you were when you began reading this book. Through reflection you have embraced who God says you are. You have opened your heart to become a woman God can use and now it is time to launch into the deep, declaring that you will no longer be silent. You were created and predestined on purpose, with purpose, for purpose. You got this. Once again I ask you to reflect on what you have read and write your response to the question, who does God say I am?

_____

_____

_____

_____

_____

_____

_____

_____

_____

_____

_____

_____

_____

_____

_____

_____

_____

_____

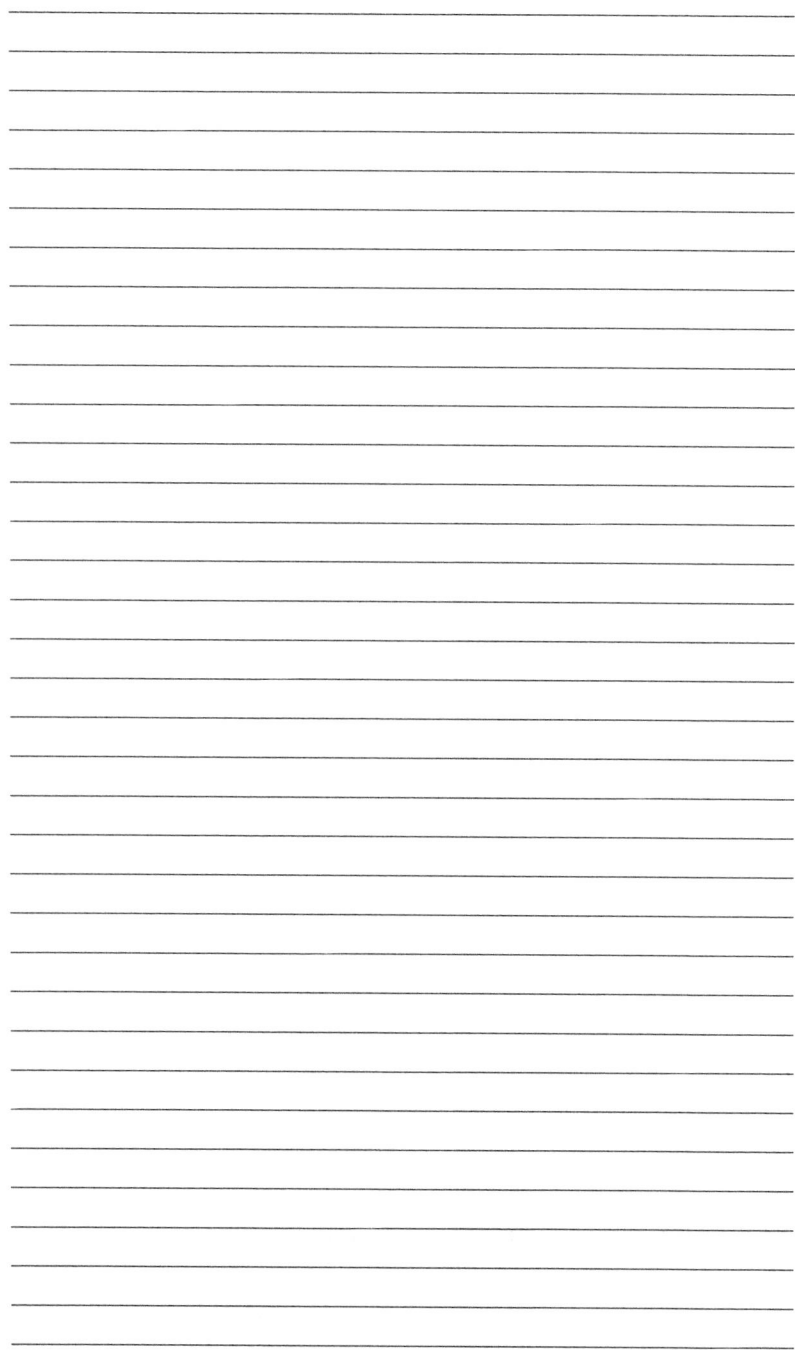

AFFIRMATIONS FOR MY LIFE

Now take a moment to search the scriptures and write affirmations declaring God's truth over your life.

_____
_____
_____
_____
_____
_____
_____
_____
_____
_____
_____
_____
_____
_____
_____
_____
_____
_____
_____
_____
_____
_____
_____

EMPOWERMENT SCRIPTURES (NLT)

- *...stand here and see the great thing the Lord is about to do. - Samuel 12:16*

- *...What is impossible for people is possible with God. - Luke 18:27*

- *And I am certain that God, who began the good work within you, will continue his work until it is finally finished... - Philippians 1:6*

- *So let it grow, for when your endurance is fully developed, you will be perfect and complete, needing nothing. - James 1:4*

- *...If God is for us, who can ever be against us? - Romans 8:31*

- *...be strong through the grace that God gives you in Christ Jesus. - 2 Timothy 2:1*

- *...Anything is possible if a person believes. - Mark 9:23*

- *...Here on earth you will have many trials and sorrows. But take heart, because I have overcome the world." - John 16:33*

- *...what we suffer now is nothing compared to the glory he will reveal to us later. - Romans 8:18*

- *... And I am convinced that nothing can ever separate us from God's love... - Romans 8:38a*

SALVATION PRAYER...Father I ask you in the name of Jesus to forgive me of my sin. I confess today that I believe Jesus is the Son of God and He was born of a virgin birth. I believe Jesus died on the cross and God has raised Him from the dead with all power. I believe the scripture to be the words given to men inspired by God. I confess Romans 10:9, 10 (NLT) which says...

> *"If you (I) confess with your (my) mouth that Jesus is Lord and believe in your (my) heart that God raised him from the dead, you (I) will be saved. For it is by believing in your (my) heart that you (I) are (am) made right with God, and it is by confessing with your (my) mouth that you (I) are (am) saved."*

Lord upon my belief and my confession I believe that *I AM SAVED!*

Write today's date _____ this is your spiritual birthday or day of renewal.

www.ingramcontent.com/pod-product-compliance
Lightning Source LLC
Chambersburg PA
CBHW062020040426
42447CB00010B/2078